MW00478511

Words Matter

Nobel Peace Prize Laureate **Kailash Satyarthi** is the first India-born, resident Indian to have been conferred with the honour.

After completing his graduation in electrical engineering, Mr Satyarthi began teaching at a university. However, soon, the desire to work for the underprivileged children compelled him to quit his job.

The issue of child rights and child labour was not yet a part of public discourse when Mr Satyarthi founded the Bachpan Bachao Andolan (BBA) in 1981. The organization has rescued more than 85,000 children from conditions of exploitative labour and modern-day slavery, and has been successful in rehabilitating them. He is confident that the worst forms of child labour will be eliminated in his lifetime.

Mr Satyarthi has organized and led many marches in India and across the world, including the Global March Against Child Labour in 1998 that saw 15 million people participate across 103 countries. He is currently leading another historic march called Bharat Yatra against child sexual abuse and trafficking. This is linked with the '100 Million for 100 Million' global march to inspire the youth to help their underprivileged brethren.

To fulfil his vision of a world free of violence against children, Mr Satyarthi has established the Kailash Satyarthi Children's Foundation. The foundation's mission is to help create and implement child-friendly policies through research, advocacy and campaigning to ensure the holistic development and empowerment of children.

Besides the Nobel Peace Prize, Mr Satyarthi is the first Indian to have been awarded the Defenders of Democracy Award, Medal of the Italian Senate, Robert F. Kennedy Human Rights Award and the Harvard Humanitarian of the Year Award, among a few others.

...BECAUSE

Words Matter

.*Selected Quotes*.

KAILASH SATYARTHI

RUPA

Published by
Rupa Publications India Pvt. Ltd 2017
7/16, Ansari Road, Daryaganj
New Delhi 110002

Sales centres:
Allahabad Bengaluru Chennai
Hyderabad Jaipur Kathmandu
Kolkata Mumbai

Images sourced from Shutterstock and
LZT/Alamy Stock Vector (Page 30)

The views and opinions expressed in this book are
the author's own and the facts are as reported by him
which have been verified to the extent possible, and the
publishers are not in any way liable for the same.

ISBN: 978-81-291-4845-2

Second impression 2018

10 9 8 7 6 5 4 3 2

The moral right of the author has been asserted.

Printed at Replika Press Pvt. Ltd, India

*Childhood is in danger except
when there is will.
Will is vain except
when there is wisdom.
And wisdom is futile except
when there is compassion.*

Contents

Freedom

Freedom is non-negotiable.

Freedom is a gift from
the divine.

Kailash Satyarthi

Let every child be free to
be a child.

When I liberate a child,
I liberate myself. Freedom
is my inspiration
and power.

I refuse to accept that the shackles of slavery can ever be stronger than the quest for freedom.

A world without childhood freedom cannot be at peace.

Kailash Satyarthi

Every child is born free
to fly in the open sky
but sexual abuse clips the
wings. Let's become the
wind under their wings.
Let's enable them to fly.

Every child is free within
himself, it is the shackles
of society which bind him.

The smile of
Freedom on
innocent Faces
is the most
rewarding

Every child should be free
to laugh and cry, free to
play and learn and free to
have a dream.

Till each child born in
India gets a free, safe,
healthy and respectable
childhood, we are not free.

Kailash Satyarthi

Childhood and freedom
are inseparable from
one another. Therefore,
childhood freedom
will prevail.

Childhood means freedom
from fear and worries.
Every child must be free
from violence, abuse
and exploitation.

...because Words Matter

In the first smile of
freedom on their beautiful
faces, I see the
gods smiling.

❧

.18.

Democracy is inseparable
from freedom, and
freedom inseparable from
childhood. Childhood and
freedom are incomplete
without one another.

❧

Kailash Satyarthi

Freedom is inevitable. Any
effort to break freedom will
break the civilization.

Slavery and civilization
cannot coexist.

.19.

Notes

_____

_____

_____

_____

_____

_____

_____

_____

_____

_____

_____

_____

_____

_____

_____

_____

Knowledge
and
Education

When the door of a classroom opens for a child, a million doors of opportunities open up.

Education leads to empowerment and plays a critical role in creating leaders.

Kailash Satyarthi

Learning is not just a legal
or constitutional right; it is
a divine right, which god
has given us all.

A mind illuminated with
knowledge is sown
with seeds of freedom
which ensure that such a
mind will not be exploited
or enslaved.

.23.

...because Words Matter

When a child writes
the first alphabet, the
script of writing a better
world begins.

Yesterday's axiom was that
you cannot not sleep in
peace if your neighbour is
hungry. But today's axiom
is that you cannot even live
or work in peace if your
neighbour is illiterate.

Kailash Satyarthi

There is no source of light
as bright as education.
One cannot imagine
any beauty in the society
without education.

Education is the key
to breaking the barriers
of inequality.

...because Words Matter

Education is not just a right, it's a remedy.

Education seeks to promote peace and tolerance, enhance options and opportunities for employment and elevate the living standards of people.

Kailash Satyarthi

The power of knowledge
begins with us and
culminates with a feeling
of *Vasudhaiva Kutumbakam*
(The world is one family).

From child marriage to
discrimination, girls too
face barriers to education.

When girls from backward
communities sit in
classrooms, shoulder to
shoulder with boys of
higher caste and class,
the script of social justice
is written.

.28.

Education is the most
powerful weapon to
break the shackles of
mental, physical and
social servitude.

Kailash Satyarthi

A little investment in
education gives
invaluable returns.

The denial of education is
the biggest scandal of
our times.

Knowledge &
Information
are the
Fulcrum of
progress

I refuse to accept that the world is so poor that even when it can bring all the children into classrooms with just one week of global defence expenditure, it fails to do so.

.32.

Where even one child is bereft of the right to education, society will not prosper.

Kailash Satyarthi

Rights, security and hope
can only be endowed
through education.

Education alone has the
potential to turn the tide
in favour of the oppressed.

...because Words Matter

Education is the
most effective way of
unleashing the limitless
human potential.

When one wall of a
classroom is built, millions
of walls that divide
humanity collapse.

Kailash Satyarthi

No country has ever achieved continuous and rapid economic growth without first having at least half of its adults able to read and write.

The road to a secular, progressive and peaceful society is paved with education.

...because Words Matter

We must invest in
education to make the
world a safer and more
beautiful place for
our children.

❧

Today, the youth are rising.
They're protesting against
injustice and inequality.
But it is happening only
where they have education.

❧

Kailash Satyarthi

It is not poverty that causes illiteracy, but illiteracy that leads to poverty.

Education is the key to end poverty for both families and countries.

...because Words Matter

When a
child picks up a
pencil, millions
of guns are
weakened

Without inclusive education, we are fighting a lost battle. The most marginalized must get access to the same quality of education as the most privileged.

Education is the wand that can clear the cobwebs of violence and ignorance.

Kailash Satyarthi

Many of the gains achieved
by education result from
the fact that it enables
people to exercise greater
choice and have more
control over the events that
shape their lives.

.41.

Education, and only
education, can create a
level playing field for a just
and equitable society.

...because Words Matter

Education is fundamental
to democracy and
transparency in
global governance.

It is time to create and use
knowledge for the benefit
of an entity that binds us
all together—children.

Kailash Satyarthi

Sustainable development is
unimaginable without an
education that fosters skill
formation, employability,
entrepreneurship, equity
and ethics.

⚜

Education for all is
imperative to safeguard the
future of our children in
war zones and situations
of conflict.

⚜

...because Words Matter

The cost of education
is little but the social
and economic benefits
are enormous.

Education should no
longer be a powerful tool
in the hands of a few, but
a fundamental right for
each one of us.

Kailash Satyarthi

Education is a value, right and power, not a market commodity. Governments must ensure free, inclusive, quality and equitable education to children.

We are accountable to each child who isn't in school today.

...because Words Matter

Inclusive education
is fundamental to
inclusive growth.

✿

.46.

As long as knowledge stays
the monopoly of the rich
and elite, we will continue
to live in a disparate world.

✿

Kailash Satyarthi

Learning is the birthright
of every human being.

Education is the driver of
economic growth.

Notes

_____

_____

_____

_____

_____

_____

_____

_____

_____

_____

_____

_____

_____

_____

Peace

Peace looks like the smiling face of a child who has just found freedom.

We can all consciously move towards peace if we prioritize children in our policies.

Kailash Satyarthi

We need pencils and
books in the hands of
our children, not tools
and guns. We need our
children in classrooms, not
in workplaces or war zones.

Denial of education is the
greatest danger to
world peace.

…because Words Matter

Peace
is no longer piecemeal
It is a global challenge
and must be
addressed collectively
with education becoming
a key
to this struggle

How can you live in peace
when millions of children
are completely denied their
childhood and freedom for no
reason or sin?
You should act.

❧

If we are to create a
non-violent world with equal
rights, we must begin with
our children.

❧

Kailash Satyarthi

If we do not change our ways, I fear we are on a collision course where violence triumphs over peace and extremism triumphs over tolerance.

Notes

Non-Violence

There is no greater
violence than to deny the
dreams of our children.

I call for zero tolerance on
violence against children.

Kailash Satyarthi

Silence against child abuse
is violence.

Child marriage is proof
that our society is still
uncivilized. It is an assault
on the mind, body and
soul of our daughters.

...because Words Matter

An act of terror on a child is an assault on the entire human civilization. Fearlessness, unity and peace together can defeat these forces.

.60.

Abuse of children is a blot on humanity.

Kailash Satyarthi

Children killed in conflicts
are not merely numbers.
Each one of them had
a face, a heart and an
innocent soul.

We have dreams but
millions of children in the
world do not. Someone,
somewhere is responsible
for that.

...because Words Matter

We must be intolerant to violence against children.

❧

The fight against the exploitation of children, and girls in particular, is a struggle against age-old mindset and complacency.

❧

Kailash Satyarthi

Breaking silence is imperative to break the age-old social taboo around child sexual abuse.

How can we justify the worshipping of goddesses when our own daughters are exploited, abused and killed every day? We must break the silence before it gets too late.

...because Words Matter

Fear
is a form of violence
If we are
living in fear,
we are
living in violence

Inequality and violence
are synonymous with
the chicken and egg
relationship. Which came
first, it is hard to say.

.66.

Each figure has a face
behind it; every data has a
cry behind it.

Kailash Satyarthi

It is the violent mindset
of few that does not
permit for the rights of an
individual to be translated
into action.

Inequality fuels violence;
violence fuels inequality.

...because Words Matter

Child exploitation,
illiteracy and poverty
form a vicious circle of
violence against children.
This circle blocks national
development and weakens
democracy.

.68.

Kailash Satyarthi

Violence is not just
manifested externally but
has been internalized in
the multiple facades of
inequality. We see civil
and political inequality,
socio-cultural inequality as
well as economic inequality
exhibiting a deep disrespect
for human rights.   .69.

Notes

_____

_____

_____

_____

_____

_____

_____

_____

_____

_____

_____

_____

_____

_____

_____

_____

_____

_____

Children

I represent here the sounds of silence, the cries of innocence and the faces of invisibility. I have come here to share the voices and dreams of our children, because they are all our children.

Every child has a name, a face and is born with certain rights.

Kailash Satyarthi

When democracy is compromised, children suffer the most.

The adult-centric development has its eyes on the next election, whereas child-centric development aims for the next generation.

...because Words Matter

Children have always been my philosophical teachers and heroes. They are the heart of human society.

⁂

If development policies are framed keeping children in mind, they automatically move away from being short-term objectives to being long-term visions and goals.

Kailash Satyarthi

Children are not the creators of war but they are its worst sufferers.

The issues pertaining to child well-being are broken into pieces which results in compartmentalization and fragmentation of policies and programmes. Let us consider all children's problems as one entity.

The measure of a society
and its Future
lies in the way
it treats its children

The state of children is
a reflection of our past,
present and future.

I challenge the passivity
and pessimism surrounding
our children. I challenge
this culture of silence, this
culture of neutrality.

Kailash Satyarthi

For all children to have
an equal opportunity
at realizing their full
potential, innovation must
reach the most marginalized
and invisible and meet their
needs and rights.

❧

Let us preserve the
innocence of children,
which is invaluable.

❧

...because Words Matter

No
power is stronger
than the moral
power
of
our children

We have been hearing the rhetoric time and again that children are the future. But why do we not understand that they are the present, they are the today, they are now?

Children cannot and will not wait. Their childhoods must be protected.

Kailash Satyarthi

We must remember that we
have inherited this world,
so we should strive to
return it to our children in
a better shape.

.83.

When we endeavour to
build a fair and just world,
the best way to begin is to
care for all children.

...because Words Matter

Let's create a free and fearless India for our children, not one for the perpetrators of crime against children.

Every single minute matters; every single child matters; every single childhood matters.

Kailash Satyarthi

Let our intellectual and moral might arrive at its rightful conclusion—our children's well-being.

A little investment in healthy childhoods will shape the future of a healthy nation.

...because Words Matter

If we fail our
          Children now,
    we will fail our
        Future forever

Change has come and no
voice is louder than our
children's.

The single aim of my life
is that every child is: free
to be a child, free to grow
and develop, free to eat and
sleep, free to laugh and cry,
free to play and learn, free
to go to school and, above
all, free to dream.

.88.

Kailash Satyarthi

Children are not only
leaders of tomorrow but
also the leaders of today.

Today, beyond the darkness,
I see the smiling faces of
our children in the blinking
stars. Today, in every
wave of every ocean, I see
our children playing and
dancing. Today, in every
plant, in every tree and
mountain, I see our children
growing freely with dignity.

...because Words Matter

Children have proved that they are the leaders of today. They have all the courage and spirit to question those in power, and they have enough wisdom and vision to provide the solution to many of the problems which adults think are complicated.

Kailash Satyarthi

Violence is not only
manifested externally,
it has its roots in the
multiple facades of
structural inequality; to
achieve peace and spread
compassion, we need the
sanctity of children—clean
and untarnished by adult
prejudice—to decide our
fates.

.91.

Notes

_____

_____

_____

_____

_____

_____

_____

_____

_____

_____

_____

_____

_____

_____

_____

Youth

I believe in the power
of change. And I know
children and youth can
lead the change the world
needs.

Whenever people have risen
against oppression and
injustice, it is because of
the youth.

Kailash Satyarthi

No segment of society
can match the power,
enthusiasm, idealism and
courage of the youth.
The power of youth is a
'commonwealth' for the
whole world.

Promises and pledges will
be of no avail if we do not
include the youth in
solution-making.

...because Words Matter

Youth dividend isn't a fuel for growth or a tool for industrial production, but, essentially, it is the moral force for an inclusive and progressive society.

.96.

India is rising because of her educated, enthusiastic and enterprising youth, mainly boys and girls from small towns.

Kailash Satyarthi

Youth are emerging as the new beacon of power and resistance. Give them a chance to channel their energy into positive change.

Let this generation of young people be the generation to end slavery.

The energy of the
youth is a force
which can move
the world towards
a better future

Even today, citizens and politicians opine that banning child labour is impossible. I debunk this myth here.

⁂

Youth is not the problem, but the solution. Their power will shape the world's future.

Kailash Satyarthi

If we save just one
generation, this generation,
then it will take care of all
the generations to come.

My dear friends, I see a
world where young people
will drive change.

...because Words Matter

Without the abolition
of child labour, many
development goals,
particularly universal
primary education, poverty
reduction and gender
equality, cannot be achieved.

Kailash Satyarthi

If we fail to harness and channel the drive of youth, their energy will turn into frustration, intolerance and violence. We must see them—and they must see themselves—as a part of the solution.

Notes

_____

_____

_____

_____

_____

_____

_____

_____

_____

_____

_____

_____

_____

_____

_____

_____

Child Labour and Child Slavery

Child labour is both
the cause and consequence
of poverty and
social exclusion.

Child labour perpetuates
poverty by depressing
adult employment.

Kailash Satyarthi

I refuse to accept that some
children are born
to work at the cost of
their freedom.

Child labour, trafficking
and slavery are not isolated
issues, and they must
be addressed in a
holistic manner.

...because Words Matter

Children born in poor families or countries are not responsible for their poverty, rather they are the victims. We further victimize them by making them work.

Daily experiences of discrimination and isolation are the heaviest burden borne by domestic child labourers.

Kailash Satyarthi

Domestic child labourers
are hidden behind doors
and are invisible to the
eyes of the society which is
responsible for
exploiting them.

Child labour is not
an isolated problem.
Trafficking is not an
isolated problem. They are
both interlinked.

...because Words Matter

Failure
to end child
slavery is our
collective Failure

The script of economic growth must be written by the decent work of adults, not by the sweat and exploitation of children.

I will see the end of child slavery in my lifetime.

Kailash Satyarthi

No country can solve the
problem of unemployment
if it cannot eradicate
child labour.

If child labour is not
addressed properly and
seriously, none of the
developmental goals can
be realized.

...because Words Matter

Elements of force, compulsion, deceit, coercion, temptation and false promises are common denominators in trafficking of innocent children.

We must remember that each day lost in the life of a child labourer is irrecoverable.

Kailash Satyarthi

The most shameful
commentary on today's
society in one sentence is:
slavery still exists and our
children are the
worst sufferers.

Slavery does not belong to
the last century, it is
still prevalent in its
cruellest forms.

...because Words Matter

Let's pledge to put an end
to the scourge of
child slavery.

Child slavery is not a
myth. It can be found
in everything—from the
clothes you wear to
the food you eat.

Kailash Satyarthi

Trafficking and slavery
are not isolated problems.
They are interconnected to
a wider spectrum of issues.

Inclusive education is not
possible if millions of
children are trapped
in slavery.

A sustainable economy and society cannot be built on the foundations of slavery.

.118.

I refuse to accept that the combined will, capacity, compassion and courage of all the nations is incapable of wiping out the scourge of child slavery.

Kailash Satyarthi

As many jobless adults
as the number of child
labourers shows the skewed
nature of employment.
Children are preferred
in jobs even when their
parents remain unemployed
because of the cheap,
docile and more vulnerable
nature of child labourers. .119.

Notes

_____

_____

_____

_____

_____

_____

_____

_____

_____

_____

_____

_____

_____

_____

_____

Law and Governance

The judiciary is the
custodian of the cumulative
moral conscience of
the society.

❧

The success of the Juvenile
Justice Law is not to be
measured by the number
of juveniles put behind
bars, but by the number
of children reformed and
rehabilitated by it.

❧

Kailash Satyarthi

There should be a clear
language on the issue
of child slavery, child
trafficking, child labour
and education.

If justice doesn't reach
the last person, inclusive
development and peace are
distant thoughts.

An ideal law
guides the way
and
doesn't dictate

We cannot let fear
permeate our society.
Justice not only needs to be
delivered, but also seen.

Let's change our political
culture—politics of
next elections to politics of
next generation.

Kailash Satyarthi

The judiciary has
strengthened our
democratic institutions
and saved millions of
marginalized children and
people of the world.

Protect our children to
protect our constitution.

...because Words Matter

Notes

_____

_____

_____

_____

_____

_____

_____

_____

_____

_____

_____

_____

_____

_____

_____

Compassion

Compassion for the world's children can be the unifying force that patches humanity's soul and puts us on the right course again.

⚜

.130.

I have read about mukti and moksha (liberation and salvation). But, in my life, I find compassion to be the connecting force of the entire universe.

⚜

Kailash Satyarthi

Businesses with compassion
is the way forward.

Ignite the spark of
compassion for children in
your heart and the entire
world will be illuminated.

...because Words Matter

The essence
    of spirituality
        is inherent
in each one of us~
    it is compassion

We are now feeling
the turbulent winds of
globalization of market
economies and technology.
I strongly urge us to
initiate a gentle breeze of
compassion to repair the
wrongs in the world.

I call for the globalization
of compassion.

Kailash Satyarthi

Light the spark of
compassion for children
to remove this darkness
of apathy, fear and
intolerance from the world.

Every heart and every door
should be open to refugee
children and not one more
child should be left to die.

...because Words Matter

The joy of living for
oneself is limited. The joy
of living for others
is boundless.

.136.

Are we connected to each
other through compassion,
which is the essence
of humanity?

Kailash Satyarthi

Businesses cannot thrive at the cost of society and ecology. They must be driven by compassionate intelligence.

Compassionate intelligence leads to constructive results while fear yields only reactionary outcomes.

...because Words Matter

If compassionate solutions
are sought in our
businesses, governments
and administrations, then
there will be more social
security and lesser fear.

.138.

Today, we must make the
world feel the pain of
millions, which you and
I represent.

Kailash Satyarthi

Businesses must ensure that no child labour is involved in their supply chains.

One should also not forget that benefits of globalization may turn disastrous with the lack of compassion.

...because Words Matter

Let us globalize the world
through compassion for
our children.

.140.

Today, we must make the
world listen to the sound
of silence, which you and
I represent.

Kailash Satyarthi

Today, we must make the
world acknowledge the faces
of invisibility, which you
and I represent.

...because Words Matter

Notes

Anger

Why can anger not be
translated and channelized
to create a better and more
beautiful, more just and
equitable world?

Anger is a power, it is
an energy, channel it for
social good.

Kailash Satyarthi

Most of my brightest ideas
came to me in a state of
anger against injustice.

Do not use anger for
revenge or hatred.

...because Words Matter

Convert your
Anger
into constructive
ideas and action

If we are confined in
the narrow shells of ego
and circles of selfishness,
then anger will manifest
itself in hatred, violence,
revenge and destruction.
But if we are able to break
the circles, then the same
anger will transform into
.148.   our greatest power.

Kailash Satyarthi

Anger is energy, it is power. And the law of nature is that energy can neither be created nor destroyed. It can never vanish; but it can be channelized to positivity.

Notes

Leadership

The strength of any
country lies in its people
and I urge you to initiate
strict action to resolve the
problems at hand.

.152.

I refuse to accept that
together we are incapable
of restoring childhood and
freedom.

Kailash Satyarthi

Leaders love obstacles
because they convert these
obstacles into success. They
solve complex problems
with simple solutions.

Let's not forget that history
is not made by those who
stand at the fence but by
those who dare to jump
into the ring.

...because Words Matter

You have a chance to be
the light dispelling the
darkness of illiteracy.

You cannot become a
leader by playing with
words. True leadership
requires translation of
words into action.

Kailash Satyarthi

Each one of you is a
champion, a change-maker.
Do not look for a hero
around you. Be your
own hero.

The strength of a leader
is not the number of
followers he's created but
the new leaders
he's inspired.

My biggest success is giving
visibility to forgotten
children.

India is a land of a million
problems, but it is also
the mother of a billion
solutions. Each one of us is
a solution to the problems
of our country.

Kailash Satyarthi

Let us create a society
where the voice of right
becomes the voice
of might.

The time has come to act
with strong will. This is the
place. And we are the ones
who will bend the arc of
history in favour
of children.

...because Words Matter

A leader
resides in each
one of you
Give yourself
a chance

The time has come for all
well-meaning and educated
people to come together in
a unified force to demystify
knowledge and take it to
the masses.

.160.

Our collective resolve
will put an end to the
sufferings of children,
forever.

Kailash Satyarthi

Let's walk together. In the
pursuit of global progress,
not a single person should
be left out or left behind
in any corner of the world,
from east to west, from
north to south.

.161.

How will the dreams of
millions of young victims
of servitude, trafficking
and other worse forms
of labour exploitation
come true? Who will help
them become leaders of
tomorrow and write their
destiny with their own
hands, if not
you and me?

Kailash Satyarthi

Notes

Notes

_____

_____

_____

_____

_____

_____

_____

_____

_____

_____

_____

_____

_____

_____

_____

_____

Notes

_____

_____

_____

_____

_____

_____

_____

_____

_____

_____

_____

_____

_____

_____

_____

Notes